K-9 TACTICAL TEAM TAKEDOWNS
AND CHOKE DEFENSE TACTICS

Blake Broadhurst

AuthorHouse™
1663 Liberty Drive
Bloomington, IN 47403
www.authorhouse.com
Phone: 833-262-8899

Because of the dynamic nature of the Internet, any web addresses or links contained in this book may have changed since publication and may no longer be valid. The views expressed in this work are solely those of the author and do not necessarily reflect the views of the publisher, and the publisher hereby disclaims any responsibility for them.

Any people depicted in stock imagery provided by Getty Images are models, and such images are being used for illustrative purposes only.
Certain stock imagery © Getty Images.

This book is printed on acid-free paper.

ISBN: 978-1-6655-0781-3 (sc)
978-1-6655-0782-0 (e)

Print information available on the last page.

Published by AuthorHouse 11/30/2020

authorHOUSE®

Strategy without tactics is the
slowest route to victory.
Tactics without strategy is the
noise before defeat.

Victorious warriors win first
and then go to war,
while defeated warriors go to war first
and then seek to win.

Sun Tzu's The Art of War

FORWARD

I am writing this book because I believe in the evolution of law enforcement and the tactical operator. Currently, law enforcement as a whole is being challenged by our society to make drastic changes in the way we operate. This is hard for us as law enforcement officers to want to move forward, since most of the concerns of the public are not the root of our problems.

To truly serve and protect our communities as professional police officers we do not need to turn our focus to campaigns on changing the perception of the police. We need to focus on evolving into and performing as professionals. This is done by consistent training and evaluation of skills. When we commit to professionalism and hold ourselves accountable to elite standards, then we will have risen up to the level of excellence expected by the people we serve.

Now that I have stepped off my pedestal, here is a little about me. I am a police K-9 handler and instructor with over a decade of tactical experience to include street crime units, swat team operations and GoJu martial arts training. I work in a major metro city, where I have been in over 100 uses of force, ranging from the deployment of every tool on my gun belt, to apprehensions with the K-9 and the use of deadly force on an armed suspect.

At my department, we have 15+ K-9 teams, with hundreds of deployments a year to include take downs, area searches, tracks and apprehension of numerous violent and sometimes un-expectedly armed suspects in all kinds of environments.

During my time as a K-9 handler and instructor, I have noticed that there is a need for skilled tactics on defending our K-9 partners from different violent encounters with suspects. As I sought out information on this subject, I found that the majority of experienced handlers did not have an effective nor efficient way of defeating violent suspects actions.

The tactics taught in this manual were developed from after action debriefs of my real-world deployments and the study of other K-9 handler's deployments from my agency as well as neighboring agencies. I used a ten-step method which is listed below to refine the techniques taught. This method allowed me to test what actually works in real world deployments and confrontations.

To bring this full circle, I wrote this training manual for the K-9 handler who is open minded with a growth mindset and wants to evolve their skills so that they can perform at a higher level in the chaotic realm of combat. This is not the end all, be all of K-9 combat tactics, these are tested options that will always be open to evolution.

As a former athlete, swat operator and current police K-9 handler and instructor, I have noticed that change is not popular. I have experienced first-hand that new, out of the box ideas are not always acknowledged or encouraged and that most of the time they are stomped out prior to even being heard.

There is a saying "with age comes experience and wisdom." While that might hold some truth, I don't believe it is an absolute. Experience is defined in the dictionary as: Practical contact with and observation of facts or events. Nowhere in this definition is there a reference to time. What comes with time is maturity. Wisdom is defined as the soundness of an action or decision with regard to application and experience. Put in laymen terms, a true tactician looks to develop their wisdom with the focus being on increasing his skill by consistently learning, analyzing, and studying of his experiences and then by putting his knowledge to the test.

That being said, true experience is won by the person who has repeatedly placed themselves in a position where they can gain working knowledge and wisdom in the subject they are pursuing. Listed below are ten steps that can be taken to help a student evolve in learning and performance.

1. Learn the basic and fundamental technique.
2. Understand the reason of **why** the techniques are deployed.
3. Practice the technique till proficient.
4. Apply in training scenarios.

5. Applying it in real time.
6. Reflect on performance of the real-time technique and what you could do better.
7. Apply technique until you have reached an automated response.
8. Reevaluate it and tailor it to your skill level.
9. Expand on it or reinvent it.
10. Explain and teach it to other.

As I look back over the years at my personal journey as a law enforcement officer, I realized that I built the foundation of my skills on practical real-world experience. I used the basics that I learned and went out into the street and applied them. Whether it was traffic stops, searches or foot pursuits. I did each skill hundreds of times until I got to an unconscious level of comfort, which allowed me to operate in any environment or situation.

Once I got to this level of experience, I actually got too comfortable and stopped striving to learn. I became over confident, which lead to the decline of my performance on the street. It wasn't until I got into a fight with an equally skilled and motivated suspect, who violently resisted arrest, that I realized I was immature in my skill, and ability to evolve.

I will always remember the statement made by the suspect that changed my life. "Is that all you got, you better up your game rookie." From this point, I sought out a mentor and committed myself to evolutionary learning and training which is obtained by using the 10 steps above.

From the above day, when I was a field training patrol officer to now a K-9 handler I have come a long way and can say that the above steps have developed my skill set and boosted my real-world experience learning to another level.

I wrote this forward to encourage the point of evolved learning and training to defeat those who have fallen into a place of stagnancy. Train hard, train smart and train to beat life as we can't cheat death.

I would also like to take the time to thank all those who have made this book possible. I want to thank my wife Lindsay for allowing me the time to complete this project. My parents David and

Daniella Ballard for encouraging me to be myself and put my ideas out into the world. My trainer Derwin Bradley for helping me develop, test and deploy the tactics. My photographers Jackie Wool and Kelsey Blackmon for the amazing photos. Ofc. Aaron Goss and K-9 Officer Elio Florin for their help with recreating the scenarios. All glory given to God.

Training Standard

The focus of this book is to improve the tactical proficiency, professionalism and performance of a police K-9 team. It is equally important to understand that as handlers we must make sure our performance is complete and in line with federal case law. The three main cases that I feel dictate our actions are:

Graham v Connor- Even though this isn't a K-9 specific case it addresses the use of excessive force in apprehending a suspect and gives a standard as well as an analysis of the totality of circumstances. This case law gives three factors that dictate the actions of a K-9 team during a takedown. 1. Severity of crime, 2. Does the suspect poses an immediate threat, 3. Is the suspect actively resisting or attempting to evade arrest by flight.

Goodman v Harris County- The use of deadly force against a suspect is unreasonable in the protection of a K-9's life, unless the handler perceives a threat to his own life. This case defines that the federal courts found that the K-9 is considered property. As it pertains to this book, martial art and precision combat tactics are taught to defeat the suspect without escalating to deadly force.

Watkins v City of Oakland CA.- The excessive duration of the K-9 bite and the improper encouragement of a continuation of the attack by officer **could** constitute as excessive force. The coordinated takedown training focuses on having a preplanned way to quickly and efficiently subdue a suspect, lessening the amount of force used, time on the bite, as well as lowering the possibility of the escalation of force by both the handler and the suspect.

Training Illustration

For the handler reading this book, I want you to view this training with an open mind. We, as law enforcement officers claim to be professionals but only a handful of us are willing to truly put in the humbling and exhausting time training to reach an elite level. I want you to envision the K-9 tactical team takedown and choke defense training through this illustration.

So, imagine yourself as an active 15-year law enforcement veteran and Doc Brown from the movie Back to the Future appears with the DeLorean time machine. As he appears, he gets out the time machine, walks up and gives you the keys to the DeLorean, then tells you that there is enough gas for one five-minute trip back to the past.

So, experienced you takes the keys and travels back 14 years in the past to talk to year one LEO version of yourself. The older you, has experienced a multitude of chaotic and dangerous calls but the most challenging and life altering was your response to a lone active shooter.

As you go back in time you met the year one LEO version of you and you tell him, "Hey, I'm the future experienced version of you, I want to tell you that you are going to be tested. You will be the first cop on scene of an active shooter. The suspect will be heavily armed and inside of a building. Upon your arrival, he will have already shot and killed multiple people and he is going to try and kill you as well. I can't give you any other details other than what I have told you. "Good luck."

Then experienced you walks away, jumps back into the time machine and heads back to the future. At this point the young inexperienced version of you is left with two choices. In the first choice, inexperienced you believes that the event is going to happen but notices that the future you is obviously alive and deduces that he survived the encounter since he was able to travel back and give you a warning of the future.

So, with that in mind he looks at the circumstances and decides to stay on his current path. He'll attend the mandatory department training, and do his usual workouts, he may go to a couple of classes and maintain his current skill level but believes that on the current path he will be fine in the future.

In the second choice, young you also believes the event is going to happen but immediately starts to science the hell out of the scenario. He understands that the incident is coming at an unknown time and decides to be prepared for it. He studies the knowns from what he was told, one active shooter suspect, inside of building, with multiple casualties.

Using the above information, he decides to tailor his training, focusing on single person entries, precision stress shooting and scenario-based training to operate at a higher level, a dominating level. He takes the knowns and becomes elite at them and he studies the unknowns so that they are familiar, and he can adapt to them.

When finally faced with the foretold incident, the version of you that chose to be elite goes into the chaotic realm of combat as an operator, performing as a professional instead of an amateur. He is still anxious, but he is calm, focused, and ready for battle. He has already been here a thousand times, he has failed in an environment where he is able to learn without the harsh consequences of real time combat. He has succeeded and built expert skill and experience which fuels his confidence and performance. He can even foresee and predict the actions of the suspect before he makes them. This is not science fiction this is warrior training for the battle.

In breaking down our encounters, we use pre-planning, back chaining and dynamic scenario training to develop our responses, mindset, performance efficiency and effectiveness. Thriving - not just surviving.

So how does this directly pertain to the K-9 tactical team takedowns and choke defense training? I want you to go back to the days of being a brand-new K-9 handler. As you completed your patrol school, you spent hundreds of hours training your K-9 to find and if warranted, bite a suspect. Upon completing your initial training, you get released onto the streets where one thing is particularly inevitable. You will have to physically apprehend a suspect.

You know this before it even happens and there is a good chance it will happen multiple times during your career as a handler, almost as if someone from the future informed you. This is where the two above choices come into play. If we decide to be truly prepared and science the possible K-9 encounters, all we need to do is study and dynamically train to build operational experience.

To do this we would start off by looking at the possible suspect's positions, actions, responses and outcomes. This is our starting point to evolving our performance as a K-9 team.

Disclaimer

The instructions and techniques in this book are based on substantial experience, practical trails and expertise in multiple disciplines. Applying these tactics while integrating a K-9 comes with inherent risks and danger, some due to the unpredictability of certain training circumstances. Anyone using the instruction and or techniques taught in this book does so entirely at their own risk and both the author and publisher disclaim any liability for any injuries or other damage that may be sustained.

TABLE OF CONTENTS

K-9 COORDINATED TEAM TAKEDOWNS

I n this block of instruction, I will be highlighting dynamic circumstances of numerous apprehension positions of a suspect and the coordinated use of a K-9 team takedown. These scenarios all involve the K-9 being released to apprehend a suspect and the actions of a handler and cover officers. The tactics focus on situations where there are hazardous factors that influence an arrest of a suspect. The tactics demonstrated will be, the takedowns of a suspect armed with a weapon readably accessible on their person, close quarter apprehension (CQA), hazardous environments, and positional K-9 engagements.

Note: Prior to conducting this advanced training with all the above parties, the techniques such as the strikes and movements need to be learned and should be trained and mastered by the handler. Prior to conducting a live takedown, assess how the K-9 apprehends a suspect. The handler should study the engagement to see patterns and behaviors while they are in the apprehension or drive phase.

Points to Consider

1. Most K-9 teams deploy to search for dangerous suspects that have fled the scene of a crime on foot. These suspects usually know that they are being pursued and have the advantage of being able to know where the team is located and when the team is coming, allowing for a possible ambush.

2. The use of pre-trained coordinated arrest efforts, allow K-9 team and cover officers to safely work together as a unit to efficiently subdue a suspect.

3. This technique places the suspect at a point of disadvantage as he is distracted with the K-9 and when taken down is in most cases in a prone handcuffing position.

4. This technique allows the K-9 to engage the suspect, the cover officers to assist in immobilizing the suspect's limbs and the handler to control and command the incident.

5. This technique enables the suspect to be immobilized and handcuffed quicker, allowing for a faster removal of the K-9, which in turn leads to a decrease in excessive force use by K-9 and officers.

6. The techniques lead to less confusion and miscommunication between the K-9 team and cover officers.

7. Builds confidence in the abilities of the K-9 team and handlers.

8. Reduced chance of K-9 engaging cover officers.

9. Increases K-9 team's professionalism and builds confidence and integrity of the team and Police K-9 community.

10. The development of these tactics were to build a standard takedown system for a K-9 team and cover officers to safely apprehend a violent suspect efficiently. The goal for the team is to work in a coordinated manner, with the focus of maintaining a mobile and tactical position of advantage over the suspect, while keeping in mind the K-9 pack mentality.

Team Takedown Cover Officer Notes

In choosing a cover officer that will be assisting my team, I always take into considerations their skill level and abilities. I also make sure that the officer is willing and up to the task of running cover for me. There have been numerous times where I did not feel it was in the team's best interest for me to run with certain cover officers.

If this happens to you, I suggest asking for another cover officer as a replacement or an addition to the search team. Depending on our relationship, I also give them a briefing of the team's expectations while searching and if we encounter a suspect.

Reference the below scenarios, I used a two-man cover team not including the handler. I did this because of the scenario's higher possibility of danger and the multiple extenuating circumstances. If you do not have a second cover officer when conducting these takedowns, that's not a problem.

On most of my deployments, I usually only take one C/O, unless I have information that the suspect is armed or has shown to be excessively violent or is of larger stature. All the below takedowns could be done with just one C/O. The only thing that would really change is that the handler would work directly opposite of the K-9 and they would take the suspect down themselves, as the C/O held lethal cover.

Section 1

TAKEDOWN OF A SUSPECT IN CLOSE PROXIMITY TO A WEAPON

cenario 1- In this scenario the K-9 team encounters the suspect and is conducting the coordinated takedown in close proximity to a weapon. The environment could be inside of a suspect's bedroom, near a vehicle, in a kitchen, gun store, or near a weapon that was discarded on the ground prior to the takedown.

Advantages of Tactic-
-Prevents the suspect from possibly arming himself prior or during apprehension.
-Creates a safe working space for the K-9 team and cover officers.
-Allows the execution of a team takedown and removal of suspect into an owned space.
-Removes suspect from a hazardous area.

Setting the Stage-
In this scenario, the K-9 team has deployed with two cover officers and they have made contact with the suspect. The suspect has committed a felony offense or is a threat to officers and is refusing to comply with commands to surrender. Prior to deploying the K-9 for apprehension, officers notice there is an accessible firearm or weapon in close proximity to the suspect. In the scenario, the suspect is not actively attempting to retrieve the weapon (knife, gun, baseball bat, ext.) but is not surrendering or distancing himself from the potential threat area.

Suspect is seated and none compliant in the vicinity of a weapon but is not attempting to arm himself.

Step 1- The K-9 team and cover officers move into a triangle formation with the K-9 on lead at the point position with the handler directly behind him. The two cover officers will be holding lethal cover positioned slightly offset and behind to the left and the right of the handler approximately 1 to 2 yards to the side and 1 to 2 yards behind the K-9 team. The environment will dictate how tight the formation will be. When making contact with the suspect, allow for the handler to control and command the scenario. The handler should communicate the weapon placement, team movement and give the suspect commands. This allows the cover officers to focus on keeping lethal coverage on the suspect. It also helps with keeping the K-9 focused on the suspect and allows the handler to work at their own pace.

K-9 team positioning and communication

Note: Depending on the environment the team can also position themselves to work from a place of cover or concealment while making initial contact with the suspect. The cover team can expand laterally to gain a tactical advantage over the suspect.

Step 2- The K-9 handler is to direct the cover officers to keep a L-bracket positioning on the suspect allowing for two lethal points of engagement if the scenario turns into a deadly force engagement. Once communicated, the K-9 handler is to direct the cover officer that is closest to the weapon to advance towards the weapon cutting off the path between the suspect and the weapon, keeping lethal coverage. This movement will be executed slightly prior to the rest of the K-9 team advancing to apprehend the noncompliant suspect.

Note: This allows for the K-9 team to have a reactionary gap to retreat if the advancement of the cover officer who is moving towards the weapon turns lethal. Over all, the distance between the suspect and the weapon will dictate this tactic.

Handler directs cover officers

Step 3- On the advancement of the team towards the suspect, the first cover officer will move into position between the weapon and the suspect. Depending on the environment, the K-9 team and the second cover officer will start to move forward to apprehend the suspect using the K-9. While moving forward it is important that the K-9 team and officers pay attention to the reactive movement of the suspect allowing them to react or possibly predict the actions of the suspect.

CO#1 and team movement to suspect

Step 4- Once cover officer #1 has moved into place blocking off access to the weapon, the K-9 team and cover officer #2 continue their approach as they would on any other deployment. Personally, I train and usually have a trusted cover officer within a 3x3 feet distance, off of my shoulder holding lethal coverage until the K-9 has bitten the suspect.

CO #1 Lethal cover positioning

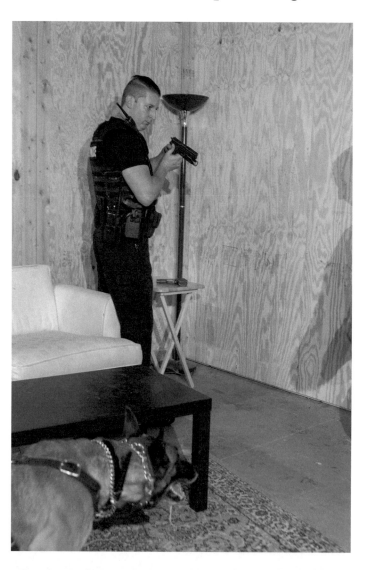

Step 5- In the picture below the K-9 has been released and engages the suspect's left forearm and the suspect continues to resist as he is still standing and actively moving. As the handler, prior to going hands on, give your K-9 and yourself a second to evaluate the positioning and the effectiveness of the bite. Once you have made that evaluation, the handler is to approach the opposite unbitten arm of the suspect at a 45-degree angle with open hands, both up near their face in a fighting stance. At this point, the suspect should be focused on the arm that the K-9 is attached to, which allows the handler to have the tactical advantage as they go hands on. The handler then grabs the unbitten arm of the suspect near the lower forearm area forcefully with his outside hand which in this scenario is his right hand.

Note: The reasoning behind the purposeful positioning of the team is to effectively and efficiently gain control of the suspect arms to subdue his movements and place him in handcuffs. With the placement of the K-9 on one arm and the handler on the opposite arm, it helps in keeping the suspect from reaching for a concealed weapon or attempting to strike or defeat the K-9.

Handler gaining arm control

Step 6- Once the handler grabs the suspect's right forearm area, he then uses his opposite arm, (left hand) to grab the suspect's right bicep/tricep area. This allows the handler to stabilize himself in an athletic position and set his feet to deliver a knee strike. While maintaining his grasp as described above, the handler is to deliver a knee strike to the suspect's right outer thigh area, aiming for the Common Peronial nerve. The use of the knee strike causes disruption in the nerve and pain compliance, allowing for the handler to gain control of the arm instead of muscling or wrestling the suspect to it. While delivering the knee strike, the handler is to start to execute an arm bar by simultaneously pulling the suspect's right wrist area with their right hand towards their waist line. The handler is to continue the technique by sliding their bladed left forearm to the suspect's tricep area to straighten out their arm. A knee strike can be delivered multiple times until you have gained the desired reaction to execute the arm bar. This allows the handler to gain control of the suspect's right arm in an arm bar with the K-9 on the left arm. As the team is executing their assignments, cover officer #2 is to stay at a readied position and orient himself in a semicircular position approximately 5 feet away awaiting instructions from the handler.

Knee Strike **Arm Bar**

Step 7- Once the K-9 team has gained control of both arms with the handler controlling one and the K-9 attached to the other, and if the suspect is still on his feet, the handler will call in cover officer #2, directing him to the position he wants him to take. This will be different depending on the appendage that the K-9 engages and I will address the positioning and movements in the next section. In this scenario, the K-9 is biting and holding on to the suspect's left arm, cover officer #2 will shift and position himself behind the handler slightly off the rear shoulder of the handler with open hands positioned chest high. When he is in position, cover officer #2 is to tap the handler on the shoulder three times and communicate verbally that he is ready and in position to transition control of the right arm from the handler to cover officer #2. When ready the handler will communicate the position switch verbally. This transition allows for the handler to switch control of the right arm to cover officer #2 who will use the arm bar technique to immobilize the arm. Once control of the arm has been given to cover officer #2, the handler is to transition to the other side and gain physical control of the K-9. Depending on the environment the handler is to move laterally, going behind the suspect to get to the K-9 positioned with their chest facing the suspect's back. For a more aggressive suspect, this allows the handler to be able to shift unnoticed into positions to deliver defensive tactic strikes to soft target areas to help in subduing the suspect. Once the handler has switched to the side of the K-9, he is to gain physical control of the K-9 by straddling the K-9's body between the handler's leg (positioned in an athletic staggered stance) and preferably grabbing the harness. This allows the handler to control the bite location and to keep the K-9 from engaging a different body part of the suspect if not necessary. It also aids in keeping the K-9 from engaging your cover officers as they are in close proximity.

CO#2 pre-transition position

Positioning of team after transition

Note: In a typical takedown where there are no extenuating circumstances (small enclosed work space, proximity to a weapon, hazardous environments) the handler and K-9 would work together to take the suspect off his feet and to the ground without transitioning a cover officer. In this scenario, a cover officer is used as a added barrier and is there to help control and remove the suspect from the area of the weapon. It also allows the handler to manipulate and control the K-9 making sure he stays locked on to the bite.

Step 8- At this point the suspect is still on his feet resisting and the K-9 has held on to the engaged left arm. The handler is positioned on the same side as the K-9 and has physical control of the K-9. Cover officer #2 is positioned on the right arm and has executed an arm bar on the suspect's right arm. On the handler's command, both him and the cover officer are to take the suspect forward off of his feet placing him on his chest in a handcuffing position. This can be done with CO#2 placing his inside leg in front of the suspect's leg, while maintaining control of the arm bar and pulling it towards the right waist band. Once the suspect has been positioned on the ground, cover officer #2 is to conduct a standing arm bar as instructed below in the training manual. The standing arm bar is a great technique that uses leverage and pain compliance to change the suspect's refusal to submit. It also allows the officer to maintain complete control of the suspect's arm while still in a standing dominant position. Once cover officer #2 secures the suspect's arm, he will communicate the execution of the lock to the handler. Cover officer #1, being lethal cover will stand by in close proximity awaiting instructions on where he is needed.

Note: If the situation dictates and there is a need to move the suspect further from a hazard, the team can escort the suspect several yards away by pulling him to either side before or after placing him on his chest on the ground.

Coordinated takedown placing suspect on chest

CO #2 conducts a standing arm bar

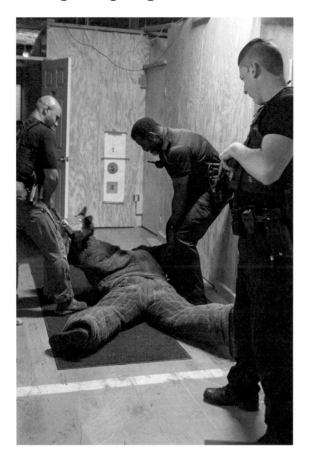

Standing Arm Bar- While the suspect is laying with their chest to the ground, the cover officer is to position himself towards the suspect straddling the suspect's arm in a standing position. The officer is to then grab the suspect's right arm at the wrist and forearm area with both hands and raise it up vertically between his legs. While doing this, the officer must simultaneously straighten the arm then lock it between his knees, maintaining the straightening of the elbow and keeping pressure and leverage at the shoulder, wrist and elbow. The use of this tactic helps the officer maintain control of the suspect's arm using pain compliance. It also allows the officer to stay in a mobile position and to access his tool belt while still controlling the suspect.

Step 9- Once CO#2 has notified handler of having control of the suspect's right arm in the standing arm bar position, the handler will call over CO#1. CO#1 is to position himself approximately 4 feet behind either shoulder of the handler. Once CO#1 is in position he is to glove up, preferably with medical gloves and when ready, taps the handler on the shoulder three times to communicate that he is in position while also saying, "Ready." CO#1 then stands by awaiting the transition of the K-9 off the bite, allowing him to secure the left arm. The handler will then remove the K-9 from the bite, while straddling him between his legs and having control of K-9's harness or collar. The positioning of the handler over top the K-9 with his elbows ups and arms horizontal to the ground like wings is key. Simotneously the handler will be holding onto the harness or collar using one or both hands depending on the way the K-9 is removed. While in this position the handler is to suitcase the K-9 for better control of the K-9's body movement as well as his bite radius. This will help with shielding cover officers from a possible unintentional bite by using the elbows as a barrier and with keeping the suspect from being unintentionally reengaged without cause. Once the K-9 has been removed the handler will reposition himself and turn the opposite direction of where CO#1 is located, still keeping an eye on the suspect in case a reengagement is needed. Once clear CO#1 is to move in and secure the arm and work with CO#2 to maintain control of the suspect's arms to complete the handcuffing. At this point the suspect has now been effectively secured and the apprehension scene now must be reevaluated.

Removal position of K-9 and handler

Final positioning of cover officers handcuffing

Step 10- Now that the suspect has been secured, take the time to open your vision and mind and reevaluate your scene and surroundings. This is where I usual take a deep breath, turn my head and eyes left and right pulling me out of the focus area of the apprehension. I scan the environment for further threats or bystanders in close proximity to me. I also communicate with my cover officers asking if they have any injuries or if there are any circumstances that I need to be aware of. I then instruct them to search the suspect's body for weapons and advice of his injuries or if necessary apply aid myself. Once the scene is secured I kennel my K-9, put on plastic medical gloves and do an injury check of the suspect, confirming the bite location and severity. I also write down and take photos of the apprehension area to better allow me to recall my environment.

Scenario 1 with leg engagement

On the above deployment, steps 1-4 would still apply and would be executed as described above. If the K-9 bites the suspect's left leg in the engagement proceed to step 5a instead of step 5.

Step 5a- In the picture below the K-9 has been released and engages the suspect's left leg and the suspect continues to resist as he is still standing and actively moving. As the handler, prior to going hands on, again give your K-9 and yourself a second to evaluate the positioning and the effectiveness of the bite. Once you have made that evaluation, the handler is to approach the same side that the K-9 has bitten which is the suspect's left leg. The handler is to approach the suspect at a 45-degree angle by stepping outwards toward the side of the K-9 with open hands, both up near their face in a fighting stance. At this point the suspect should be focused on the leg that the K-9 is attached to but this doesn't always give the advantage to the handler. A possibility is that the K-9 might have hold of the pants and not the actual leg. The difference in the approach by the handler on this apprehension is that the suspect is able to use both his arms to fight back, which allows the suspect to deliver effective strike to the handler and K-9. That being said the handler must approach with speed and aggression positioning himself behind the suspect just to the left side of him. Once in position the handler then grabs the left arm of the suspect near the lower forearm area forcefully with his outside hand which in this scenario is his left hand. After capturing the suspect's left arm, the handler is to raise his right arm high at a 90-degree angle to deliver a sweeping Shuto strike. The sweeping Shuto is a controlled extension strike and will be executed in a horizontal motion going up the shoulder with first contact being made with the trapezoid area of the suspect using the bladed forearm of the handler. The handler then forcefully extends and pushes his right forearm to the lower jaw area of the suspect to turn his head the opposite way. This causes nerve disruption and keeps them from being able to look in your direction. This will also allow for the suspect to be stunned and for the handler to gain control on an arm bar.

K-9 on leg and handler controlling arm

Step 6a- After delivering the Shuto strike as described above, the handler is to then transition his right arm down to the suspect's left tricep area above the elbow joint. The handler must keep his right forearm and hand bladed while sliding down to the suspect's tricep. While executing the above move, the handler is to simultaneously pull the suspect's wrist with his left hand towards his waist and straighten the suspect's arm with his right arm by putting pressure above the suspect's tricep and locking out the elbow joint.

Shuto strike as a distraction

Transition to arm bar

Step 7a- Once the handler has gained control of the suspect's left arm and the K-9 is still engaged on the same side leg. The handler will signal to cover officer #2 to position himself on the uncontrolled side of the suspect, which in this case would be the right side. C/O #2 can immediately apply an arm bar if the suspect is pliable allowing him to gain control of his arm. If the suspect is actively resisting then a knee strike can be delivered to the suspect's outer thigh as a distraction to gain the arm bar.

Cover officer #2 controlling arm

Note: If a knee strike is delivered, the team must be ready to immediately direct the suspect to the ground. I have found thru training and real-time application that it usually causes the suspect's leg to give out causing him to fall to the ground.

Step 8a-At this point the suspect is still on his feet resisting and the K-9 is still engaged on his left leg. The handler is positioned on the same side as the K-9 and has physical control of the suspect's arm. Cover officer #2 is positioned on the right arm and has executed an arm bar. On the handler's command, both him and the cover officer are to take the suspect forward off of his feet placing him on his chest in a handcuffing position. This can be done with CO#2 placing his inside leg in front of the suspect's leg while maintaining control of the arm bar and pulling it towards the right waist band.

Note: If the team is having a hard time taking the suspect to the ground and placing him on his chest, the handler should maintain the arm bar and can deliver a left leg inverted kick to the back of the suspect's left leg just over the calf area. This will break the suspect's base and allow the team to control him to the ground. This tactic will be determined by the location of the K-9's bite. It is preferred that the K-9 has a lower ankle bite or a hi thigh bite to deploy this strike. This is a controlled strike so as to not interfere with the K-9 or injury him.

Inverted Kick to place suspect on ground

Step 9a- Once the suspect has been positioned on the ground, the handler and CO#2 are to conduct standing arm bars as instructed earlier in the training manual. Once they both secure the suspect's arms, CO#2 can deploy his handcuffs and coordinate with the handler to complete the process. I suggest that CO#2 deploys the handcuffs rather than the handler so that the handler is able to transition to control his K-9 if needed. Once handcuffed the handler will transition to straddle and remove the K-9 from the leg bite. Cover officer #1, being lethal cover will stand by in close proximity awaiting instructions on where he is needed.

Note: If the K-9 has a positional bite where he is located on the inside of the suspect's legs it will place him in an area where if the suspect is taken to his chest he will land on the K-9. If this happens, the handler must recognize this and redirect the suspect taking him down to his back and putting him in a supine position. From there the handler can continue to flip the suspect over and place him in a handcuffing position.

Section 2

TEAM TAKEDOWN OF A SUSPECT WITH A CONCEALED WEAPON

Scenario 2- This scenario is focused on the apprehension of a suspect that is in possession of an unseen weapon but is not actively armed with the concealed weapon such as a firearm, knife or tool. To clarify the scenario further, if the K-9 team encounters an actively armed suspect where the officers have prior knowledge of the suspect being armed or the suspect is an active lethal threat, it is no longer a K-9 involved call and should be handled by the lethal cover officers in the appropriate manner to protect the team and public. This tactic is to be used when a team has engaged a suspect with the K-9 actively apprehending him and they find he has a concealed weapon on his person but is not attempting to arm himself to fight back against the team.

Advantages of Tactic-
-Allows the team to coordinate and safely subdue the arms of a suspect, keeping him from retrieving a weapon and possibly averting the escalation of the incident to the use of deadly force.
-Gives each team member a specific job to execute, thus limiting confusion allowing for a quicker and more effective takedown of the suspect.
-Allows the team to safely remove the weapon without allowing the suspect to out muscle or maneuver the officers.
-Uses the high pressure of the k-9 bite as pain compliance and a diversion as well as a tool to keep the suspect's hands from reaching for the weapon.

Setting the Stage-

In this specific scenario, the K-9 team has encountered and challenged a felony suspect which has refused to surrender. Prior to releasing the K-9, the handler assesses the situation and scans the suspect's body to identify any possible threats but does not see nor has he been threatened with a weapon by the suspect. The handler then releases the K-9 for apprehension. Once the K-9 has bitten the suspect, the handler starts to make his approach to assist in the takedown. As he makes contact with the suspect, the handler observes a concealed weapon on the suspect's body but perceives that during the resisting the suspect has not made an attempt to retrieve or use the weapon. This scenario most likely happens when encountering burglary suspects that have stolen firearms or suspects that reside in high drug and violent crime areas. These weapons could be inside of a backpack, waistband or on their ankle. The handler must use their training, experience and perception to make the decision to use lethal force or to continue with the K-9 coordinated team takedown. This takedown does not replace the righteous response of an officer using a lethal weapon or tactic.

Note: This scenario is taught with the K-9 making contact with a standing suspect, biting and holding on to their arm. An explanation of steps to take when the K-9 engages the suspect's leg will be listed at the end of this section.

Standing not actively armed suspect that has a concealed weapon

Note: For teaching purposes, the weapon is in plain view not concealed as explained above and the decoy has his back turned towards the team to illustrate the weapons position.

Step 1- The handler has released the K-9 and the K-9 has bitten the suspect's left arm, actively holding it. The handler has already evaluated the circumstances and does not see any weapons so he decided to join in the engagement. As the handler approaches the suspect from the rear, he notices there is a firearm concealed in the suspect's lower back in the waistband area. The handler must immediately notify cover officers, while moving to the suspect's right arm to gain control. The handler and K-9's focus is to pin both of his arms as a team to keep the suspect from retrieving the weapon.

Handler and K-9 engage suspect as a team

Step 2- To gain control of the suspect's arm quickly and efficiently the handler needs to over whelm the suspect and use pain compliance strikes to soften up the suspect's resistance allowing the handler to gain control. The handler is to position himself behind the suspect just off of his right side. The handler then grabs the suspect's right wrist area with his right hand and straightens the suspect's arm out pulling it towards his waistband. Simultaneously the handler is to place his left hand between the suspect's right elbow and shoulder area to balance himself. Once the handler is in position, he is to deliver a knee strike aiming for the suspect's right outer thigh making contact with the Common Peronial Nerve. This strike can be repeated numerous times until the handler has gained the desired compliance.

Delivery of knee strike to gain arm compliance

Step 3- After delivering the knee strikes and gaining control of the suspect's arm, the handler then places him in an arm bar. The arm bar technique has been described throughout the book, refer to the prior sections if needed. At this point the handler is in control of the right arm and the K-9 has a hold of the left arm. This tactic keeps the suspect's arms pinned and away from any concealed weapons.

Handler conducts an arm bar which controls both of the suspect's arms

Step 4- Once the team has gained control of the suspect's arms, the handler calls in cover officer #1. Depending on the environment if possible C/O #1 should move to the opposite side of where the K-9 is engaged and set up behind the handler slightly off his outside shoulder. In the picture below, due to the environment C/O#1 moved into position just inside the shoulder of the handler placing him closer to the K-9. The purpose of the opposite outside movement of C/O#1 is to place him in position to transfer control of the right arm of the suspect from the handler to the cover officer with the least amount of exposure to the K-9. The key to a smooth transition is communication, once the handler calls in C/O #1 the C/O must make physical contact with the handler. The most preferred way would be tapping the handler on the shoulder that the cover officer is closest to three times. The cover officer is to then verbally let the handler know he is ready to transition control of the arm.

C/O 1 moves to transition position to control suspect's arm

Step 5- Once the handler has traded off the right arm bar to C/O#1, he is to shift his position and move towards the K-9. The handler then moves into position to straddle the K-9 to gain positive control by the harness or collar. At this point, both of the suspect's arms should be controlled and C/O#2 (lethal cover) can move into a position where he can effectively engage the suspect if forced to. Usually we have the lethal cover facing towards the suspect's weapon which allows him to see if the suspect reaches for it. Once everyone is set in position, the handler and C/O#1 can move forward simultaneously. As they move forward holding both arms, the team is to pull the suspect forward off of his feet and on to his chest in a controlled manner, placing him in a handcuffing position. When placing the suspect on the ground the suspect should not be forcefully thrown to the ground. The controlled manner is used to make sure the C/O and the K-9 maintain their grip on the suspect's arms.

Cover officers move into takedown position

Step 6- Once the suspect has been taken to the ground and placed on his chest, the team is to maintain control of the suspect's arms. The K-9 should still be engaged on the suspect's left arm with the handler straddling the K-9 with positive control on the harness or collar. C/O#1 should be conducting a standing arm bar on the right arm, which has been taught in prior sections. The standing arm bar works great in this scenario because it allows C/O #1 to maintain control of the arm while still being able to access and deploy his weapons if situation escalates. Once the handler is confident that the suspect's arms are controlled, he will call C/O#2 to holster his weapon move towards the suspect's legs. If C/O#2 was not positioned behind the suspect and needs to move towards the legs. C/O#2 should move behind C/O#1 allowing for a safer transition while not being in the K-9's engagement space. When in position, C/O#2 will kneel down and take control of the suspect's legs. C/O#2 must grab the suspect's feet and cross the legs at the ankles. While crossing the ankles, C/O#2 is to move forward slightly straddling the legs while bending the knees of the suspect back towards his buttocks. Once C/O#2 has the technique locked in, he can use his chest to maintain pressure on the legs. He can also go hands free to either help handcuff or retrieve the weapon depending on its location. The above instruction will be at the handler's discretion and will depend on the amount of resistance given, the surroundings and teams skill. At this point while maintaining the standing arm bar, due to his positioning C/O#1 is now responsible as the lethal cover. Even though C/O#1 is lethal cover he does not have to have his firearm out as long as the suspect is controlled and not reaching for a weapon.

Team coordinated arrest positions

Step 7- Once all the team members have control of their assigned appendage, the handler will communicate to C/O#2 to remove the weapon. When the weapon is removed, the handler will communicate to the cover officers and the suspect that he is going to remove the K-9 and will direct the suspect to place his hand behind his back or have C/O#2 retrieve the left arm to place him in handcuffs. Depending on the location of the weapon it can be remove prior to taking the K-9 off the bite or after. If the weapon is located in a backpack, front waistband or ankle I suggest handcuffing the suspect first. If the weapon is located in the lower back area, I recommend removing the weapon before handcuffing to eliminate any confusion or opportunity for the suspect to retrieve it.

Removal of weapon by C/O#2

K-9 has been removed and C/O's handcuff suspect

Scenario 2 with leg engagement

Setting the stage- This brief instruction is for the same type of scenario as described earlier in the section but instead of the K-9 engaging the suspect's arm, he engages their leg. In the photo above, the handler has already released the K-9, assessed the situation and has engaged to assist in the takedown. When conducting a team takedown of a standing active resisting suspect that involves your cover officers, the handler must position himself to effectively control the K-9 and the suspect. When taking down a standing suspect with a K-9 that has engaged their leg, the handler should go to the same side the K-9 is engaged on. This is done so that the handler can work independently on one task but still as a team with the K-9. The positioning will allow for the K-9 to see the handler and vice versa. This will also let the handler be able to go hands on with the K-9 or create a safety barrier for the cover officers to help with the takedown.

Advantages of tactics-
-Allows handler to watch and work together on same side as the K-9.
-Creates a safe working space on opposite side of suspect for cover officer.

Step 1- As shown in the photo below the handler has released the K-9, assessed and positioned himself on the same side as the K-9. The handler has moved behind the left shoulder of the suspect, notices the concealed weapon and communicates the threat to his team. The cover officers have positioned themselves to the opposite side of the handler. Their assignment is to watch the suspect's right-hand movements and react the suspect's action if he attempts to retrieve the weapon, otherwise they await instructions. While the K-9 is still engaged on the leg, the handler uses his left hand to grab the suspect's left wrist area while simultaneously loading a Shuto type movement using his right arm. The Shuto in this case is not to be used as a direct strike but as a forceful extension of the bladed boney part of forearm. The handler is to extend the suspect's left arm across the handler's chest, pulling the suspect's left wrist towards the handler's left waistband area. Simultaneously the handler is to extend his right arm and use a bladed right arm Shuto movement. The movement should run up the suspect's upper arm and shoulder with constant pushing pressure to the side of the suspect's lower jaw area. This is NOT a strike, it is a movement to place the suspect off balance allowing handler to capture the left arm conduct an arm bar.

Handler and K-9 working on the same side of suspect

Step 2- Once the handler is ready he will call in C/O#1 who will gain control of the suspect's right arm. Depending on the level of active or aggressive resistance by the suspect, C/O#1 can deliver a knee strike to the Common Peronial nerve located in the thigh area. This strike will serve as a distraction to gain control of the suspect's right arm. C/O#2 now moves to a position where he can best take lethal coverage. When everyone is set in position, the handler will communicate with C/O#1 to move forward simultaneously to take the suspect off his feet. As they move forward holding both arms, the team is to pull the suspect forward, off of his feet and on to his chest in a controlled manner, placing him in a handcuffing position. If the suspect attempts to stay mobile C/O#1 can conduct a front trip by stepping forward with his left leg and placing his left foot inside the suspect's right foot. When placing the suspect on the ground, the suspect should not be forcefully thrown to the ground. The controlled manner is used to make sure the C/O and the K-9 maintain their grip on the suspect's arms.

Handler and C/O coordinate forward takedown

Step 3- Once the suspect is on his chest in a handcuffing position the handler and C/O#1 can both conducted the standing arm bar and coordinate the handcuffing. As soon as the suspect is handcuffed the handler immediately transitions to remove the K-9 from the engagement. The cover officers can then remove the concealed weapon and emergency medical services can be notified to respond.

Section 3

SUSPECT ENCOUNTERED IN CONFINED OR HAZARDOUS ENVIRONMENT

Mobile Removal

Scenario 3- On this takedown the K-9 team has made an apprehension of a suspect in confined or hazardous area. This takedown differs from the others as both cover officers are involved in gaining control of the suspect's arms. They will both assist in transporting and subduing the standing or kneeling suspect while the K-9 is engaged. This tactic poses an increase dynamic to the takedown due to the communication and movement of cover officer #2 in close proximity of the K-9 team with an active resisting suspect. This technique's deployment will depend on the environment and circumstance that the K-9 team encounters after biting a suspect. The scenarios can range from confined environments where the suspect cannot be placed in a prone position to the removal of a suspect from a hazardous working area. Examples of these problematic work areas would be a gathering crowd that surrounds the team, water hazards such as a pool or riven, railroad tracks, busy roadways or elevated areas with fall risks such as stairs or baloneys.

Advantages of tactic-
-Allows the team to safely transport suspect away from a hazardous environment in a secure manner.
-Allows team to move the apprehension location to a predetermined area to finish the coordinated takedown.
-Puts team in a safer environment with less unknown factors that could influence the takedown in the suspect's favor.

-When using the tactic of pulling a suspect out by the lead with K-9 attached to suspect, it allows for the suspect to fight the K-9 or access a weapon. The below tactic allows for immediate hands on when transporting.

Setting the stage-

In this scenario, the K-9 team has deployed with two cover officers and they have made contact with a suspect that has committed a felony offense. The suspect is either a threat to officers and or is actively refusing to comply with commands to surrender. Prior to deploying the K-9 for the apprehension, officers notice there is hazardous environment or a lack of work space that could place the team as well as the suspect in further danger. This can apply to a suspect who is apprehended near a railroad track, pool, ravine or on a stairwell. The below stages will depict the apprehension of a suspect that was located in a small space and is standing up.

Note: This is somewhat of an out of the box tactic since in most deployments with an apprehension the suspect is placed in a prone handcuffed position prior to removing the K-9 from the bite. In this scenario, the tactic may be a better alternative, as it allows the team to move the suspect and the arrest location to a safe working environment. This tactic may negate the possibility of dangerous environmental factors influencing the arrest. The photos below depict the suspect being apprehending in a standing position in a small space, but multiple hazardous environments can be interchanged. This technique would be used to remove a standing or kneeling mobile suspect back from an area which poses hi risk to the suspect and K-9 team. The more common alternative to this tactic would be pulling the suspect out of the danger area by using the lead while the K-9 is attached to the suspect.

Step 1- The handler has released the K-9 and the K-9 has bitten the suspect's right arm, actively keeping hold of it. The handler has already evaluated the circumstances and is aware of the lack of work space and or the hazardous environment. Prior to moving in on the suspect, the handler communicates to the cover officers that they will be conducting a "mobile removal." This tells the cover officers they will both be going hands on to help move the suspect to a safer handcuffing location. Upon communicating the takedown tactic, the handler goes directly to the K-9 and gains control of the harness or collar. It is important that the handler maintain positive control and close proximity to the K-9 as a barrier of protection for the cover officers.

Handler positions himself to gain control of K-9

Step2- Once the handler has gained control of the K-9, he will position his body as a barrier between C/O#1 and the K-9 and will lift his arms in a wing like position as shown in the picture below. This creates a safety barrier if the K-9 disengages the suspect to engage the cover officer as he moves in. Once in position the handler will call in C/O#1 to move and gain control of the suspect's left arm. C/O#1 will grab the suspect's wrist with his left hand and place his right hand above the elbow while pulling the suspect arm back slightly towards his waist. As expressed throughout the manual, if the suspect refuses to allow the cover officer to gain control of his arm the officer can deliver a knee strike as a distraction to obtain the arm. In the below photo the cover officer gained the arm immediately. Once both arms of the suspect are controlled C/O#2 moves in position. He moves directly behind the suspect approximately two feet behind and in between the handler and C/O#1 then awaits instructions. When ready, the handler calls in C/O#2 to move to his inside shoulder. While conducting the mobile removal the handler must maintain the arm and body barrier for both cover officers to safely transition into his position.

C/O#1 moves in and gains control of suspect's left arm

Step 3- Once in position the handler will communicate with C/O#2 that he is ready to remove the K-9. This would be a great time for C/O#2 to put on glove to avoid exposure to blood. C/O#2 will then stack up off the handler's left shoulder at an arm's length distance and tap the handler three times on the left shoulder to signify that he is ready to transition to the suspect's arm. The handler will then position himself in between C/O#2 and the K-9 by turning his back towards C/O#2. The handler will then remove the K-9 and start to position himself to create a protection barrier and exit path. To help create a protection barrier for the cover officers, the handler must keep his arms raised up parallel. The handler then positions his elbows in a wing type manor at the level of the K-9's head. This will limit the K-9's engagement area if he decides to attempt to reengage the suspect or officers. For the next step the footwork and movement of the handler is important. The handler will then step outward with his inside leg. In this case it would be his left leg, keeping his elbows up and distancing the K-9 team from the suspect. C/O#2 will then gain control of the suspect's right arm. The cover team should now be in control of the suspect and can either remove the suspect from the hazardous area or handcuff him then remove him. Once the K-9 team has exited and is at a safe distance, the handler is to pivot inward and turn to face the suspect, never completely turning his back to the cover team. This positioning is just in case the K-9 is needed to be released to reengage a fighting suspect who has broken free from the cover team.

K-9 Removal and barrier movement

Cover officers handcuff or remove suspect

Note- For a leg bite of the above scenario the positioning is the same. The only difference is the handler would gain control of the same side arm that the K-9 engaged on. The handler would call in C/O#1 to get the opposite arm and they would proceed to handcuff the suspect. The handler then notifies C/O#2 to get into position and the handler would then transition to the K-9 to start the removal and exit movement. For the suspect that is engaged by the K-9 and is laying on the ground needing to be removed out of a hazardous area, the handler goes straight to the K-9 and gains control to keep the K-9 from reengaging. If the team has two cover officers and the suspect is bit on the leg the handler calls in both cover officers to grab the suspect's arms and pull him towards a safe location. If the bite location is on the arm, the handler gains control of K-9 and a cover officer grabs the other arm. They then pull the suspect to a safe location and continue the steps to the coordinated takedown of a prone suspect.

K9 CHOKE DEFENSE TECHNIQUES

While researching and developing this curriculum I contacted numerous police K-9 handlers from different agencies. I specifically talked with the handlers that experienced a deployment where the suspect tried to choke their K-9. I gathered the K-9 and handler's physical attributes, experience and training. I then asked details of the choke deployment and how they defeated the suspect. What I learned was the handlers were unprepared with a point of defense and usually deployed impact weapons or used fist strikes. Their strikes typically made contact with the hard target areas on the suspect, such as the top of the head or large muscle groups. In my experience and in the combative realm, these strikes can look excessive and yield little affect in changing the suspect's behavior or actions. Mav1's tactics and takedowns focus on using proven precision strikes to soft target areas of the body to gain maximum compliance with minimal amount of force. It is to be noted that a officer cannot use deadly force to save a K-9's life, unless the handler themselves feels that their life is threatened by the suspect's actions.

In this block of instruction, I will be highlighting the most common apprehension positions of a suspect who has gained the physical advantage over the K-9 that has been released to make the apprehension. These scenarios involve the K-9 being released to apprehend a suspect and the suspect placing the K-9 in a choke to defeat, injure, or kill the K-9. The four choke positions that will be highlighted are: standing front facing/supported, standing rear supported, mount and guard positions.

Points to Consider

1. Per Federal Case law; Goodman vs Harris County, it is unreasonable for a police K-9 handler to use deadly force to protect a K-9's life unless the handler perceives his own life is threatened. The federal courts defined that the K-9 is considered property.

2. The use of a firearm aimed and fired at an appendage with the intent to wound a suspect to force him release the choke on the K-9 is still considered deadly force.

3. During off lead deployments and direct apprehensions, a suspect has the opportunity to place the K-9 in a choke position in an attempt to defeat the K-9. In most deployment to apprehension scenarios the K-9 is the first to make contact with the suspect.

4. These techniques focus on breaking the choke quickly and takes the suspect's attention off of the K-9 to keep him from reengaging the choke.

5. The technique allows the handler to scale the amount of force used to defeat the suspect. It uses evolving defensive strikes in response to the suspect's increasing or decreasing resistance level, which in turn keeps the handler from using excessive force.

6. The techniques are easily learnable and use simple tactics that can be applied under stress which coincide with most use of force polices.

7. The techniques use the same tactics and procedures for all the choke defenses, which aids in the learning process as it keeps all the scenario responses consistent.

8. Using these techniques decreases the likelihood of the handler and K-9 getting injured from the use of closed fist strikes to durable areas of the suspect's body

9. The liability to the handler and K-9 unit is lessened as the use of these techniques lower the chance of excessive force and negative perception.

10. The techniques allow the handler to defeat the choke, enable the K-9 to reengage, and place the suspect on the ground in a handcuffing position.

11. During these violent engagements, the suspect will be focused on defeating the K-9. This allows the handler the opportunity to deliver strikes and use tactics to defeat the suspect's action while he is distracted and vulnerable.

Note: Prior to conducting this advanced training with K-9 team and the decoy, the techniques such as the strikes and movements need to be learned and should be trained and mastered by the handler. Prior to conducting a live takedown, assess how the K-9 apprehends a suspect. The handler should study the engagement to see patterns and behaviors while they are in the apprehension or drive phase.

DEFENSIVE TACTICS TERMS DEFINED

In learning the defense to the listed chokes, I am going to start off by defining each common martial arts strike technique and soft target area used to defeat the actions of a suspect.

Shuto- In martial arts a Shuto or a bladed hand strike is a strike using the part of the hand opposite the thumb (from the tip of the pinky finger to the wrist) while the hand is made ridged. It is familiar to many people as a karate chop (in Japanese, *Shutō-Uchi*).

Arm Bar- A joint lock where the elbow is hyperextended in order to cause pain and compliance.

Arm Drag- Technique by which you grab suspect's arm just below the wrist with two hands then straightening the arm out by pulling it towards yourself. This is used to pull the suspect's torso in a desired direction.

Soft Targets- These are the areas on the body that when struck with force cause immediate disruption of the suspect's actions. Using these points of contact will efficiently and effectively reduce the time a suspect is resisting.

Common Peroneal Nerve- Nerve located in the lower leg that provides sensation over the posterolateral part of the leg and the knee joint.

Radial Nerve- The nerve and its branches provide motor innervation to the arm muscles, wrists and hands.

Brachial Plexus Nerves– The network of nerves located on side of neck that sends signals from your spinal cord to your shoulder, arm and hand

Note: The below photo demonstrations were done with a decoy K-9 due to the amount of time and stress that would be placed on the K-9 to take the photos. The positions and techniques have been trained in a real-time training environments with success. When training live with the handler, K-9 and decoy, safety is of the utmost importance. While training these tactics make sure to utilize the proper equipment, seasoned decoys and mature K-9s.

Section 4

STANDING REAR SUPPORTED POSITION

The suspect is in a standing position facing away from the handler and has the K-9 pinned against the wall in a choke position. The suspect has both of his hands around the K-9's neck and has lifted him off of the ground and is using a wall to help support the weight of the K-9 in an attempt to defeat or choke him.

Advantages of Tactic-

-Allows the handler to engage the suspect from the suspect's blind spot.

-Allows the handler to create distance between the suspect and wall which opens working space for team.

-Takes suspect off of his feet with minimal effort from the handler.

Setting the Stage-

The suspect pictured above, dressed in black has refused to comply with commands and is actively resisting your attempts to arrest him. The K-9 has already been released to apprehend the suspect but the suspect gained the advantage and placed the K-9 in a front choke. The suspect has positioned himself by standing with his back towards the handler, focused on the K-9 and has both hands around the K-9's neck. The suspect has lifted the K-9 off of his feet and has pinned him up against the wall in a choke. The suspect is using the wall as a brace and gravity to advance the cutting off of the K-9's airway.

Note: These steps are given for the handler that approaches from the right side of the rear facing suspect. If suspect is approached from the left side, all the directions are opposite of the ones given below. Also, while engaging the suspect with these tactics verbal commands must be given.

Step 1- While the suspect has his back turned away from the handler and his attention to defeating the K-9, the handler is to approach either side of the suspect from a 45-degree angle. In the below photo the handler is approaching the suspect from the right side. The handler then glides forward closing the distance between him and the suspect. As the handler moves forward, he must ready the lead arm into a position to execute a Shuto strike using the blade portion of the forearm. The strike will start from an upright position as illustrated in the photo below and will be executed in a downward motion with a rigid open hand (a close fist would work too.) The point of impact is the handler's bladed side of the right forearm to the suspect's right forearm just below the wrist. This first strike is used to help break the grip of the suspect's choke to the K-9 and is to be execute with force and precision which helps cause disruption to the Radial nerve. When the loosening or the breaking of the grip happens, the weight and movement of the K-9 will likely help the K-9 to get back into the fight and or out of the choke position.

Handler engages suspect and breaks their grip by using a Shuto strike

Step 2- Once the handler has delivered the Shuto strike with the right arm, he is to step forward with the rear leg, (in this case it would be the left leg) placing his left foot behind the suspect's right heel. Immediately after the handler has made contact with the strike, he is to slide his right forearm downward perpendicular to the suspect's forearm and gain control of the suspect's right wrist with the handler using his right hand. This will aid in defeating as well as keeping the suspect from reengaging the choke on the K-9 if it was broken from the Shuto strike. As the handler reaches that positioning, he is to grab the suspect's wrist and pull it towards the right side of his waist. Simultaneously the handler delivers a left arm Shuto strike with force, making the point of contact the blade side of the handler's left forearm to the suspect's right mid forearm. This strike will help loosen his grip as it affects the Radial nerve running down the arm.

Frontal view of handler gaining wrist control and delivering Shuto strike

Step 3- Whether or not the suspect has released the grip on the K-9, The handler is to secure the arm bar by maintaining the tight grip of the suspect's right wrist and bracing the handler's left arm by grabbing the shoulder area. The handler then delivers a knee strike using which ever leg is comfortable. The point of contact is the handler's knee to the suspect's Common Peronial nerve that runs down the side of his thigh. This strike is used as a distractor and softens up the suspect's standing structure. If necessary the handler can repeat the strike until the desired effect is reached or the suspect complies.

Handler delivers knee strike

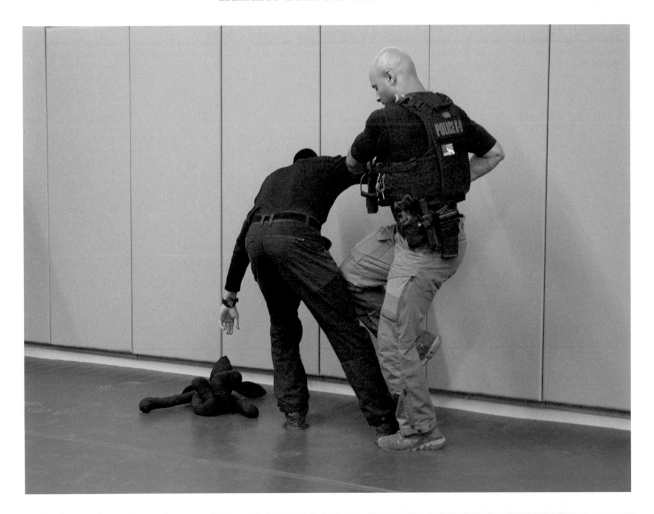

Step 4- Once the knee strikes have been delivered, the handler must maintain his grip of the suspect's right wrist and shoulder area as shown below. The handler then delivers a left leg inverted kick to the suspect's upper right calf area. The inverted kick is executed by launching the left leg with the point of impact being the suspect's upper calf area just below the hinge of the right knee. The handler is to use the inseam of the foot to make contact with the suspect's right upper calf. This causes the suspect to lose the standing base of the right leg, allowing the handler the opportunity to take the suspect to the ground. After delivering the inverted kick, the handler must maintain his grip of the suspect's right wrist and shoulder and pull him backwards towards the ground.

Handler delivers inverted kick

Step 5- Once the suspect has been pulled backwards off of his feet and is on his back on the ground, the handler will be positioned just off to the suspect's right side, the handler must use both hands to grab the suspect's right arm by the wrist area extending it straight towards the handler's body. This sets up an arm drag to place the suspect on his chest in a handcuffing position.

Handler gains wrist control to conduct an arm drag

Step 6- The handler is to pull the suspect towards him extending their body and then step with his right foot towards the head of the suspect while maintaining control of the suspect's right arm. The handler then walks towards the suspect's head in a semicircular pattern, while pulling his arm straight towards the handler's waist, using it as leverage to turn the suspect on to his chest using an arm drag.

Handler pulls the suspect over to his chest using an arm drag

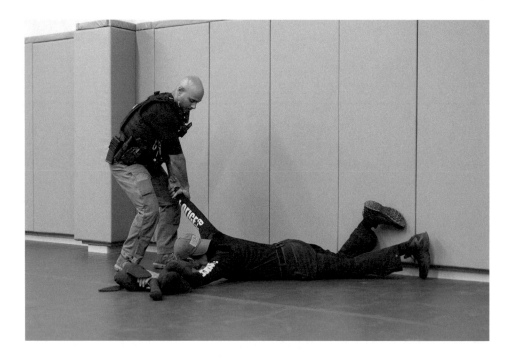

Note: K-9 engagements- I have found that in real time apprehensions and training scenarios that if the K-9 is able and mature, he will stay in the fight. Keep in mind if the suspect is taken down and is in a supine positioned on his back, the handler and K-9 will have to work together. In most cases I have found that the K-9 will circle away from the handler. This is due to the K-9 not wanting the handler to suitcase and out him. To get a smooth transition of the suspect to a prone position the handler may have to maintain the arm drag but step directly over and across the suspect towards the K-9. This should force the K-9 to walk the suspect's arm towards his head which would cause the suspect to turn to his chest.

Step 7- Once the suspect has been turned over with his chest to the ground, the handler is to maintain control of the right arm and straighten it out. The handler then steps forward, lifts the suspect's arm vertically and proceeds to lock the suspect's arm between his knees using the standing arm bar. This allows the handler to easily hold the suspect in prone positioning with pain compliance until a cover officer arrives, as well as address alternate threats advancing towards them while in a dominate and mobile position. While in this position the handler can maintain the arm bar and compliance of the suspect, while keeping his head on a swivel and if necessary can un-holster and utilize a tool. Once the suspect is placed in this position they are to be handcuffed and if the K-9 is still engaged he can now be removed and medical attention can be given to the suspect.

Note: This would be the juncture that we would incorporate the coordinated K-9 takedown highlighted in the earlier sections utilizing your cover officer and or cover team.

Standing arm bar

Section 5

STANDING SUPPORTED FRONT CHOKE POSITION

The suspect is standing with his back against a wall supporting himself, facing the K-9 team in an attempt to defeat or choke the K-9.

Advantages of Tactic-

-Allows handler to break the choke quickly while disrupting suspect's nervous system.

-Depending on the resistance of the suspect, the tactic can be scaled to a higher or lower level of force.

-Uses three to four different strike points to gain compliance and break the grip and attention of suspect.

Setting the Stage-

The suspect in the picture above, dressed in all black has refused to comply with commands and is actively resisting your attempts to arrest him. The suspect has positioned himself by standing with his back supported against the wall facing the K-9 team. The K-9 has already been released to apprehend the suspect, but the suspect has gained the advantage and placed the K-9 in a front choke. The suspect has both of his hands around the K-9's neck and is lifting him off of his feet. He is leaning back on the wall to help him support the weight of the K-9 and gravity to advance the cutting off of the K-9's airway.

Step 1- Handler must face the suspect and position himself at a 45-degree angle to either side of the suspect as shown below. As the handler gets to that positioning, they must have both hands up with their hands open and their feet should be staggered. The left leg should be in front of the right in an athletic stance. Strong side back, assuming a good fighting stance.

Note- These steps are given for the handler that approaches from the right side of the front facing suspect. If suspect is approached from the opposite side all the directions are opposite of the ones given below. Also, while engaging the suspect with these tactics verbal commands must be given.

Handler is prepared with hands up and has positioned himself at 45-degree angle

Step 2- The handler glides forward closing the distance between him and the suspect. As the handler moves forward, they must ready the lead arm into a position to execute a Shuto strike using the left forearm. The strike will start from an upright position as illustrated in the photo below and will be executed in a downward motion with a rigid open hand. The point of impact is the handler's bladed side of the lead forearm to the suspect's left forearm just below the wrist. This first strike is used to help break the grip of the suspect's choke to the K-9. When the loosening or the breaking of the grip happens, the weight and movement of the K-9 will likely help the K-9 to get back into the fight and or out of the choke position.

Handler is prepared to engage the suspect by delivering Shuto strike.

Step 3- Immediately after the handler has made contact with the lead left hand Shuto strike, they must slide their forearm in a forceful downwards motion, perpendicular to the suspect's arm. The handler must keep contact with the suspect's left arm until they reach their lower wrist area with their hand. This will aid in defeating as well as keeping the suspect from reengaging the choke on the K-9, if his grip was broken from the Shuto strike. As the handler reaches that position, which is illustrated in the photo below, he then grabs the suspect's wrist to control the arm.

Note- Whether the suspect has lost the choke on the K-9 and or the K-9 has reengaged, go ahead and follow thru with the rest of the stages necessary to subdue and place the suspect into a handcuffing position.

Handler delivered a Shuto strike to the suspect's forearm and has slid down to his wrist to gain control

Step 4- Simultaneously, while executing step 3, the handler should be loading their right arm in a high pre-Shuto strike position as illustrated below. The handler should also be in an athletic staggered stance with their lead foot and knee slightly bent and the rear leg stepping forward positioned behind the suspect's left heal.

Delivery of the second Shuto strike to suspect's forearm

Step 5- Execute the right arm Shuto strike with force, making the point of contact the blade side of the handler's right forearm to the suspect's left mid forearm. This strike will help loosen his grip as it affects the Radial nerve running down the arm. After completing the strike, maintain control of the suspect's wrist with the left hand. **Note:** A closed fist can also be used in placed of a bladed open hand.

Delivery of second Shuto strike and foot placement of handler behind heel of suspect

Step 6- If the hold on the K-9's neck has been broken, maintain control of the suspect's left wrist while straightening out the suspect's left arm towards the handler's left hip pocket. The handler must then place their right forearm, leveraging it above the left elbow of the suspect to conduct an arm bar. As the handler secures the arm bar, he must pull the suspect towards him using their arm and deliver a knee strike. The strike can be delivered with either leg to the suspect's mid-thigh area to the Common Peroneal nerve that runs vertically down the leg. This strike can be repeated multiple times and is used as a distraction as well as a pain compliance. It will also soften the suspect's posture, allowing for an easier transition to defeat the choke or place the suspect in a handcuffing position.

Note: If the grip is unbroken even after the above step, the handler must maintain control of the suspect's arm. The handler is to slide their left hand up to the crease of the suspect's bent left arm and grab it, then with their right hand they are to place it on the shoulder/collar area of the suspect. The handler then delivers another the knee strike while pulling the suspect towards themselves as the strike is delivered. By changing the grip and stance it will allow the handler to deliver a more powerful and effective strike, this should collapse the suspect's stance or take them off their feet causing them to fall to the ground. If the suspect still has the K-9 in a choke the handler is to proceed to upscaling which is explained further down in the section.

Delivery of one or more knee strikes

Step 7- If the above steps enabled the handler to break the grip of the suspect and free the K-9 from the choke, proceed to breaking the suspect down to place him in a handcuffing position. After delivering the second Shuto strike described in step 5 and delivering the knee strike described in step 6, the handler must execute an arm bar to take down. This is done by pulling the suspect's left arm towards the handler's left waist band extending the suspect's left arm straight while keeping the suspect's hand towards the handler's body or left hip pocket. While doing this, the handler must slide the blade of his right forearm to the suspect's left outer forearm. The placement would be just above the elbow joint allowing him to lockout the suspect's left arm. At this point the handler should have three points of contact with the suspect 1. wrist, 2. elbow and 3. right foot inseam blocking the suspect's left heal.

Noted: If properly trained after the K-9 has been released from the suspect's grip the K-9 should reengage and help the handler by drawing attention away from the arm bar and to the K-9's bite. This would allow the K9 team to work together and the handler to execute the tactics easier.

Execution of the arm bar

Step 8- Once the handler has placed the suspect in the arm bar, he is to maintain the technique while stepping forward with the right leg that was located behind the suspect's left heal. The handler then needs to place his right leg in front of the suspect's left shin and plant his foot. By executing this step while leveraging the arm bar forward across the handler's body it should place the suspect in a prone position with the handler still in control of the suspect's arm.

Front trip of suspect while maintaining arm bar

Step 9- Once taken to the ground, the handler is to maintain control of the arm bar while staying on his feet. The handler has to step forward, then lift the suspect's arm vertically proceeding to lock his arm between his knees conducting an standing arm bar. This allows the handler to easily hold the suspect in prone positioning with pain compliance until a cover officer arrives, as well as address alternate threats advancing towards them while in a dominate and mobile position. Once the suspect is placed in this position they are to be handcuffed and if the K-9 is still engaged he can now be removed and medical attention can be given to the suspect.

Note: Depending on the level of aggressive resistance by the suspect and if the suspect still has an unbroken grip around the K-9's neck, stage 6 is the up-scaling point. I made mentioned earlier that using these techniques allow the handler to scale the amount of force used to subdue the aggressive suspect. If the first two Shuto strikes work in defeating the choke, then the handler will progress from step 1 thru step 9 to get the suspect in a prone position to handcuff them.

Handler has placed suspect in prone position and has placed him in a standing arm bar

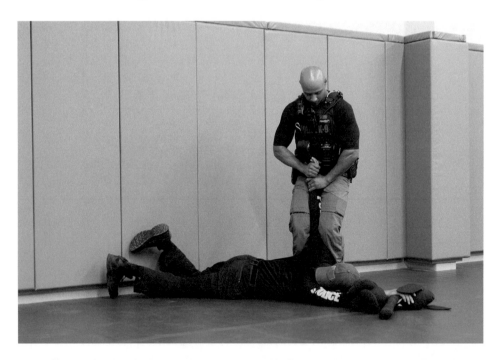

UPSCALE CONTINUATION OF FORCE TO DEFEAT CHOKE

If the handler has progressed thru stages 1 up 6 and the suspect still has the choke on the K-9, the handler must advance and scale upward his use of force until the choke is defeated. The handler is to go from step 6 and skip to step 10.

Step 10- If the suspect still refuses to stop their attack on the K-9 after steps 1-6 have been executed, the handler is to maintain hold of the suspect's left wrist. The handler is to then pull it tight towards their waist and then deliver a quick right handed, upward thrusted, Shuto strike. Conducting a brachial stun, making contact with the outer neck area, which causes a disruption in the suspect's actions and mental functions. This also places the handler's right hand in position to cup the suspect's chin just by turning their palm inward and their right leg should still be staged behind the suspect's left heel. If this strike works to break the choke the handler will be in prime position to conduct a rear takedown and should proceed to Step 11, if not and the suspect continues to aggressively resist proceed to Step 10a.

Upwards Shuto brachial stun

Step 10A- Once the handler has executed steps 1-6 then up scaled to step 10 and still needs to elevate his level of force, the handler is to let go of the cupped chin and the suspect's wrist simultaneously. The handler then twists at his core and immediately deliver an upward left forearm or elbow strike with his left arm with the point of impact being handler's forearm or elbow to the suspect's chin.

Note: At this point we must keep in mind that the suspect is continuing aggressively resist to defeat or kill the K-9, so our strikes must be delivered with speed and aggression to defeat the suspect's actions and save the K-9's life.

Delivery of left forearm strike

Step 10B- After the handler delivers the left forearm or elbow strike, he is to extend the same left arm in a continuous flowing motion and conduct a Shuto strike making contact the suspect's Brachial nerve located on the neck as illustrated below, using the forearm to engage a collar hold to aid in forcing the suspect forward to the ground.

Shuto strike to the suspect's Brachial nerve, setting up a forward collar takedown

Note: <u>Go back to step 9</u> Once the suspect is on the ground depending on their positioning, the handler can execute the final steps that proceed to handcuffing. If the suspect is positioned with their chest towards the ground, the handler must gain control of the suspect's left arm with both his hands and can go back to step 9 (standing arm bar) to finish handcuffing process as illustrated below.

Step 9- Standing arm bar

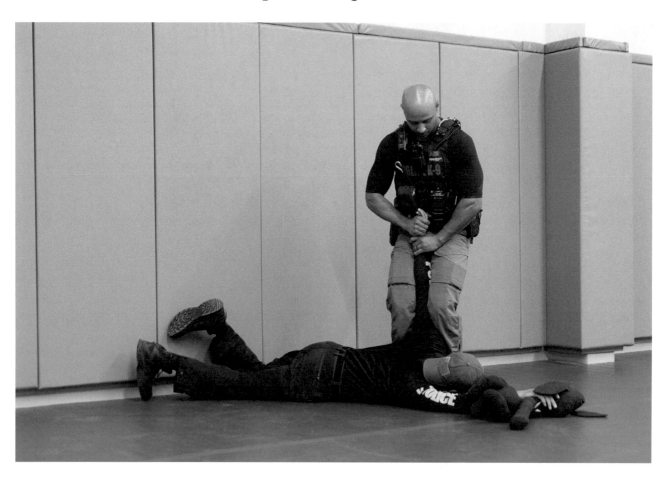

Steps to follow if the suspect was taken down using a back trip and is in a supine position with his back on the ground.

Step 11- Once the handler has cupped the suspect's chin, he is to twist his upper body to his right side. The handler then pulls the suspect backwards and keeping his right leg in place behind the suspect's heel, causing him to fall backwards and land on his back. While doing this, the handler must make sure to maintain control of the suspect's left arm as they fall to their back. The handler must also focus on staying on their feet. This will help in repositioning the suspect to their chest to place them in a handcuffing position.

Back tripping the suspect to place them on the ground

Step 12– Once the back trip has been executed and the suspect has been taken to the ground the handler will be positioned just off to the suspect's left side, he must then use both hands to grab the suspect's left arm by the wrist area, extending it straight towards the handler's body.

Suspect has fallen to his back the and handler is setting him up to turn him to his chest

Step 13- The handler is to pull the suspect towards him extending their body and then step with his left foot towards the head of the suspect while maintaining control of the suspect's arm. The handler then walks towards the suspect's head while pulling his arm straight towards the handler's waist, using it as leverage to turn the suspect on to his chest using an arm drag. The finishing position will be the same as in step 9 with the locking of the arm with the knees in a standing arm bar, placing the suspect in a handcuffing position.

Handler using the arm drag to turn the suspect to his chest into a handcuffing position

Go back to the below step to handcuff

Step 9-Finishing handcuffing position

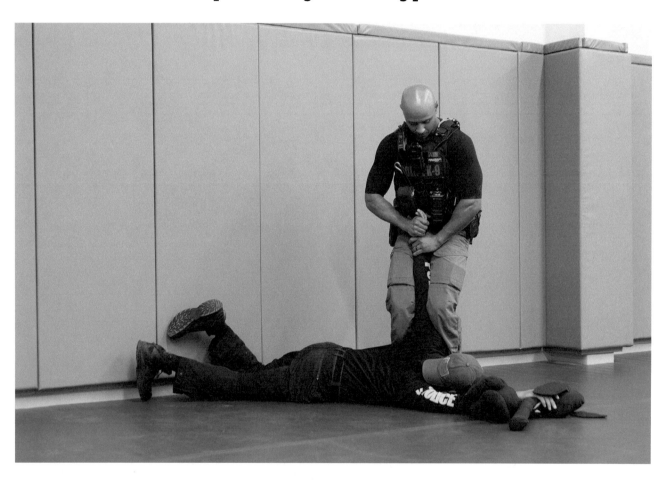

Section 6

GUARD CHOKE POSITION

The suspect is laying on his back in a guard position with the K-9 on top of him with his hands around the K-9 neck or his arms around K-9's body attempting to choke or defeat the K-9.

Advantages to Tactic-
-Allows handler to stay in a mobile position on their feet, enabling the use of counter movements to the suspect's actions or environment.

-Allows handler the use of their tool belt. (chemical agent to soften the suspect's resistance or firearm for lethal circumstances.)

-The handler is able to observe the suspect's hands to see any actions of the suspect that would escalate the level of force.

Setting the Stage-
The suspect pictured below refused to comply with commands and is actively resisting your attempts to arrest him. The K-9 has already been released to apprehend the suspect but the suspect has gained the advantage and placed the K-9 in a choke while on his back in a guard position. The suspect has positioned himself with his back on the ground and both of his arms or hands around the K-9 neck or body.

Guard Choke Position

Note: These steps are given for the handler that approaches from the right side of the rear laying upward facing suspect. If the suspect is approached from the opposite side, all the directions are opposite of the ones given below. Also, prior to engaging, the handler must quickly evaluate the suspect to see if there are any visible hazards or weapons accessible to the suspect. As the handler engages the suspect with these tactics, verbal commands must be given continuously.

Step 1- The handler is to approach with his both hands up in an open handed defensive position and as he closes the distance between himself and the suspect, the handler is to lower his body position using his right hand to grab the suspect's right wrist. The handler's left hand is to be placed on the suspect's right upper shoulder allowing the handler to brace himself and load a right knee to conduct a strike.

Handler makes contact with suspect and positions himself to deliver a knee strike

Step 2- Once the handler has braced himself by positioning his hands, he needs to slightly rolls the suspect forward while maintaining hold of his wrist. The reasoning for this is to expose the suspect's lower rib area to be able to deliver a right knee strike. The handler is aiming for the floating rib. This strike can be delivered multiple times till compliance or a break in the K-9 choke has been reached. While delivering this strike, the handler is to transition his left-hand position to the suspect's right wrist, grabbing the wrist with both hands so that he is roll the suspect to expose his rib area. The handler then has to pull the suspect towards him while delivering the strikes and breaking the choke.

Handler delivers knee strike while maintaining his grip on the suspect's arm

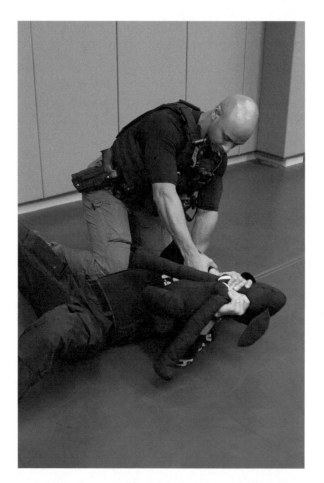

Step 3- Once the handler has broken the choke grip of the suspect he is to maintain control of the suspect's right wrist with both hands. The handler then elevates his stance, getting up in an athletic staggered stance with the left foot staggered towards the head of the suspect and the right foot split behind towards the suspect's waist.

Handler breaks the suspect's grip and takes athletic stance

Note: It is to be noted that during these scenarios the suspect will be focused on defeating the K-9. This allows the handler the opportunity to deliver strikes and use tactics to defeat the suspect's action while he is distracted and vulnerable.

Step 4- The handler, while maintaining control of the suspect's wrist with both hands then steps forward with their right leg past the head of the suspect continuing to step forward until the suspect has been pulled over to his chest placing him in a handcuffing position. At this point the K-9 should have reengaged the suspect, helping the handler by distracting him as he is places the suspect in handcuffs.

Note: The positioning of the K-9 will vary depending on their reaction to the turning of the suspect. The handler may have to pull the suspect outwards in a circular movement or step over his chest to better place him in a prone position.

Handler maintains the arm of the suspect and turns him over into a handcuffing position

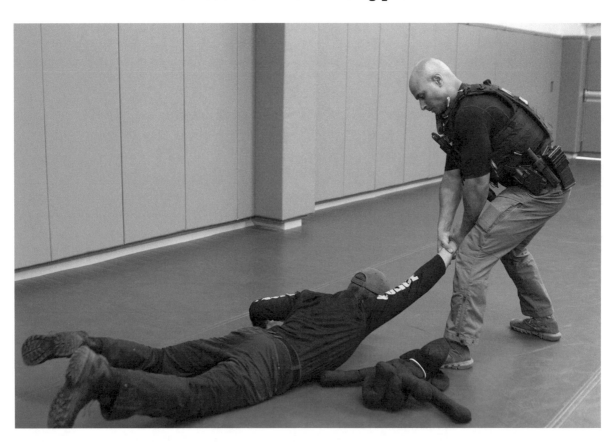

Step 5- Once the suspect has been turned over with his chest to the ground, the handler is to maintain control of the right arm and straighten it out. The handler then steps forward, lifts the suspect's arm vertically and proceeds to lock his arm between his knees into standing arm bar. This allows the handler to easily hold the suspect in prone positioning with pain compliance until a cover officer is called to assist. It also allows for the handler to address alternate threats advancing towards them while in a dominate and mobile position. While in this position the handler can maintain the arm bar and compliance of the suspect, while keeping his head on a swivel and if necessary can un-holster and utilize a tool. Once the suspect is placed in this position they are to be handcuffed and if the K-9 is still engaged he can now be removed and medical attention can be given to the suspect immediately.

Note: This would be the juncture that we would incorporate the coordinated K-9 takedown highlighted in the earlier sections, utilizing your cover officer and or cover team.

Handler executes a standing arm bar

Section 7

MOUNT CHOKE POSITION

T he suspect is in a mount position on his knees on top of the K-9 facing away from the handler and has the K-9 pinned against the ground in a choke position. The suspect has both of his hands around the K-9's neck in an attempt to defeat or choke K-9.

Advantages to Tactic-

-Allows handler to engage either side of the suspect's mid section as well as both sides if nessasary.

-Keeps the handler in a mobile position allowing for freedom of movement and access to tools.

-Allows handler to disengage and repostition himself if suspect presents alternate threat.

Setting the Stage- The suspect in the picture below, dressed in all black has refused to comply with commands and is aggressively resisting your attempts to arrest him. The K-9 has already been released to apprehend the suspect but the suspect has gained the advantage and placed the K-9 in a mounted choke. The suspect has positioned himself on top of the K-9 and has pinned him against the ground. The suspect has placed his hands around the K-9's neck or collar with his focus being on defeating the K-9.

Mount Choke Position

Step 1- Handler must position himself perpendicular to the suspect and approach the middle torso area. Once in position the handler will approach with both hands up and with open palms. His feet will be staggered with the handler's left leg in front and the right leg slight offset behind it in an athletic stance.

Note: These steps are given for the handler that approaches from the left side of the suspect. If the suspect is approached from the opposite side, all the directions are opposite of the ones given below. Also, while engaging the suspect with these tactics verbal commands must be given.

Handler approaches the suspect lining perpendicular with his torso

Step 2- The handler is to engage the suspect by grabbing and bracing himself with his left arm, placing it near the left shoulder area of the suspect. The handler simotaneously does the same with the right arm but places his hand above the lower back area of the suspect. Once the handler has made physical contact with the suspect and has executed the arm placements, he is to deliver a knee strike to the suspect's rib cage area. The handler can deliver numerous strikes until the desired behaviour of the suspect has been reached.

Hands placement and knee Strike

Step 3- Once the handler has received the desired reaction from the delivered knee strikes and the suspect is no longer resisting or choking the K-9, the handler then transitions to place the suspect in a handcuffing position. The handler now changes his body position back to a staggered athletic stance and his hands to a arm bar postion. The handler then grabs the suspect's left wrist with his left hand and pulls it back to the handler's left waist band area, while straightening the suspect's arm. The handler simotanelusly uses his right hand and places it just below the suspect's tricep, using it as a leverage point to straighten out the suspect's arm.

Transition to a arm bar

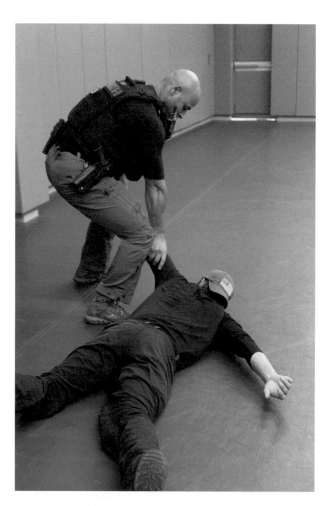

Step 4- Once the suspect's arm has been straightened out, the handler is to maintain control of the left arm by holding on to the suspect's wrist with one hand and his palm with their other hand. The handler then steps forward, with their left leg, while lifting the suspect's arm vertically and proceeds to lock his arm between his knees executing a standing arm bar. This allows the handler to easily hold the suspect in prone positioning with pain compliance until a cover officer is called to assist. It also allows for the handler to address alternate threats advancing towards them while in a dominate and mobile position. While in this position the handler can maintain the arm bar and compliance of the suspect, while keeping his head on a swivel and if necessary can un-holster and utilize a tool. Once the suspect is placed in this position they are to be handcuffed and if the K-9 is still engaged, he can now be removed and medical attention can be given to the suspect immediately.

Note: This would be the juncture where we would incorporate the coordinated K-9 takedown highlighted in the later chapters utilizing your cover officer and or cover team.

Locking in a standing arm bar

K-9 Apprehension Report Details

When writing apprehension reports we must paint a vivid and descriptive picture of our experience during the incident. This allows the attorneys, judges, jurors, supervisors and the public to feel what we felt and have a better understanding of why we made the decisions at hand. A lot of the time, we tend to not realize that as K-9 handlers we are exposed to and perform in a realm with a higher level of chaos and danger. We need to make sure that we document and explain our decisions and actions by utilizing the art of storytelling, specifically giving details, observations and facts. Below are just some report details that can be included in an apprehension report.

1. Crime(s) committed
   - Level of offense (Mis/Fel)
   - Aggravating circumstances.

2. Weapons involved in the crime or that were accessible during the apprehension.

3. Reason for deployment of the K-9.
   - Search, takedown, protection

4. Documented time of:
   - Crime
   - Deployment
   - Locating of the suspect
   - Active search

5. Location of scene and where the suspect was found.

6. The distance from the scene where suspect fled to his apprehension location.

7. Notation of opportunity to surrender prior to apprehension.
   - perimeter being established
   - marked units with lights and helicopter
   - number of statements made by officers to stop resisting or surrender

8. Description and number of suspects.

9. Direction of travel.

10. The exact K-9 announcements made.
    - How they were made (PA, loud voice)
    - Number of announcements given.
    - If no announcement were given state why.
    - Example "Police K-9" suspect description "come out with your hands up and surrender or we will release the dog and find you and you could be bit."

11. K-9 Behavior exhibited during search (human odor characteristics.)

12. Articles found during the search and their location.

13. Challenge statement given, and the number of times stated.
    - Response of suspect.
    - Environmental or hazardous factors influencing the suspects ability to respond.

14. Location details of where the suspect was found.
    - Lighting
    - Cameras
    - Environment
    - Visibility
    - Obstacles
    - Potential hazards

15. Actions of the suspect.
    - No response
    - Level of resistance
    - Statements made
    - Physical breathing

- Eye movement
- Fleeing posture

16. Bite location, injury extent, reengagement (laceration, scratches.)

17. Notification made to supervisors and the response for medical treatment (Fire rescue, hospital suspect was admitted to.)

18. Unintentional bite and circumstances that lead to the bite.

19. Any additional strikes given and person that handcuffed.

20. Statements made by the suspect and witnesses that observed the apprehension or actions of suspect.

21. Commands given during apprehension and how handler outed the K-9 (bite, release)

22. Identity of suspect and the positive identification by the victim or witness.

23. Willingness of victim to press charges and positively identify suspect.

24. Any video available to review chase, body cam, surveillance.

25. Deployment considerations and bite explanation. Give a numbered recap of your reasons for deployment and apprehension.

   "It is to be noted prior to deploying the K-9 the following factors were taken into consideration:"
   - Crime and Severity
   - Fears (in fear for public, officers)
   - Weapons used, possessed and accessible
   - Suspect movements and statements

- Environment and hazards
- Past actions of suspect
- Possible violent or negative outcomes if action isn't taken
- Type of resistance

26. Apprehension and tactics considerations. Give a numbered recap of what you considered prior and during the incident.

"Prior to apprehending and handcuffing the suspect the following factors were taken into consideration:"
- Number of opportunities to surrender and warnings given
- Actions that elevated your concern for safety
- Your perception and concerns
- The suspect's acknowledgement of LEO presence and commands
- Prior expense of physical effort and tiredness
- Suspect's attributes, experience and skill level
- Tactics used to decrease the possibility of the use of excessive or deadly force

Printed in the United States
By Bookmasters